A GIFT FOR:

mom

FROM:

Clinton

DATE:

5/11/03

Crazy About My Mom

BARBOUR
PUBLISHING

CRAZY ABOUT MY MOM™

ART AND DESIGN BY JACKSON DESIGN COMPANY
SILOAM SPRINGS, ARKANSAS

ISBN 1-58660-853-3

PUBLISHED BY BARBOUR PUBLISHING, INC., P.O. BOX 719, UHRICHSVILLE, OHIO 44683,
www.barbourbooks.com

Member of the
Evangelical Christian
Publishers Association

PRINTED IN CHINA.

Crazy About My Mom

FINALLY, ALL OF YOU SHOULD BE
OF ONE MIND, FULL OF SYMPATHY
TOWARD EACH OTHER, LOVING ONE
ANOTHER WITH TENDER HEARTS
AND HUMBLE MINDS. ~St. Peter

1 PETER 3:8 NLT

I'M CRAZY ABOUT MY MOM
BECAUSE SHE DOESN'T
ACT HER AGE.

I'M CRAZY ABOUT MY MOM
BECAUSE SHE LOVES
ALL MY ARTWORK.

I'M CRAZY ABOUT MY MOM
BECAUSE SHE UNDERSTANDS THAT
SOMETIMES A KID GETS DIRTY.

I'M CRAZY ABOUT MY MOM
BECAUSE SHE KNOWS HOW TO MAKE
A BAD DAY GET BETTER.

I'M CRAZY ABOUT MY MOM
BECAUSE SHE LETS ME
PICK OUT MY OWN CLOTHES.

(USUALLY.)

I'M CRAZY ABOUT MY MOM
BECAUSE SHE UNDERSTANDS
OUR NEED TO EAT HEALTHY STUFF.

I'M CRAZY ABOUT MY MOM
BECAUSE SHE STAYS NICE AND CALM
AT MY SOCCER GAMES.

I'M CRAZY ABOUT MY MOM
BECAUSE SHE DOESN'T MIND
STAYING UP LATE TO HELP ME
WITH MY HOMEWORK.

And you knew about this assignment when?

Are you sure that's OUR mom?

I'M CRAZY ABOUT MY MOM
BECAUSE SHE LOOKS
BEAUTIFUL ON DATE NIGHT.

I'M CRAZY ABOUT MY MOM
BECAUSE SHE HELPS DAD TO CALM
DOWN WHEN I'M IN TROUBLE.

I'M CRAZY ABOUT MY MOM
BECAUSE SHE GETS US
EVERYWHERE ON TIME.

I'M CRAZY ABOUT MY MOM
BECAUSE IT'S EASY TO BUY
GREAT GIFTS FOR HER.

I'M CRAZY ABOUT MY MOM
BECAUSE SHE HELPS ME WIN
THE BATTLE AGAINST GERMS.

I'M CRAZY ABOUT MY MOM
BECAUSE SHE KNOWS WHERE
EVERYTHING IN THE HOUSE IS.

I'M CRAZY ABOUT MY MOM
BECAUSE SHE REALLY GETS
INTO THE HOLIDAY SPIRIT.

I'M CRAZY ABOUT MY MOM
BECAUSE SHE LIKES TO STAY UP
LATE ON FRIDAY NIGHTS AND
WATCH MOVIES WITH US.

I'M CRAZY ABOUT MY MOM
BECAUSE SHE BELIEVES THAT
CLEANLINESS IS NEXT TO GODLINESS.

I'M CRAZY ABOUT MY MOM
BECAUSE SHE CAN MAKE
BOO-BOOS GO AWAY.

I'M CRAZY ABOUT MY MOM BECAUSE
SHE HAS HER OWN SPECIAL WAY
OF MAKING ME FEEL PROTECTED.

I'M CRAZY ABOUT MY MOM
BECAUSE SHE'S SO BRAVE —
SHE'S NOT EVEN AFRAID
OF WILD ANIMALS.

I'M CRAZY ABOUT MY MOM
BECAUSE SHE'S SUCH A
GOOD SNUGGLER.

I'M CRAZY ABOUT MY MOM
BECAUSE SHE MAKES SURE I STAY
WARM ON A COLD WINTER DAY.

Now you come right back in
if you get too cold out there.

And THEN what happened?!

I'M CRAZY ABOUT MY MOM
BECAUSE SHE STAYS INFORMED
ABOUT WHAT'S GOING ON
IN THE WORLD.

I'M CRAZY ABOUT MY MOM
BECAUSE SHE IS
A GREAT ENCOURAGER
WHEN I GET A LITTLE SHY.

I'M CRAZY ABOUT MY MOM
BECAUSE SHE DOESN'T GET TOO MAD
IF I MISS THE SCHOOL BUS.

I'M CRAZY ABOUT MY MOM
BECAUSE SHE'S FUN TO SHOP WITH.

I'M CRAZY ABOUT MY MOM
BECAUSE SHE TRUSTS ME
ENOUGH TO LEAVE ME ALONE
WITH MY GIRLFRIEND.

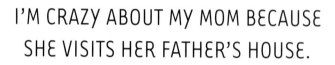

I'M CRAZY ABOUT MY MOM BECAUSE
SHE VISITS HER FATHER'S HOUSE.

I'M CRAZY ABOUT MY MOM
BECAUSE SHE DOESN'T MIND
GETTING UP EARLY —
EVEN ON SATURDAYS.

Hey mom, what time did you say
we can leave for the park?

Okay, at three I pick you up from school and we head to the orthodontist... then I take your brother over to basketball practice... we have to finish your science project tonight... then I have a meeting at...

I'M CRAZY ABOUT MY MOM
BECAUSE SHE CAN REMEMBER
EVERYTHING THE WHOLE
FAMILY'S GOT TO DO.

I'M CRAZY ABOUT MY MOM
BECAUSE SHE'S AS CREATIVE
AS THE LADY ON TV.

And you made this with leftover paper towel rolls and empty egg cartons?

I'M CRAZY ABOUT MY MOM
BECAUSE SHE MAKES SURE
I HAVE EVERYTHING I NEED
TO SUCCEED AT SCHOOL.

I'M CRAZY ABOUT MY MOM
BECAUSE SHE ISN'T AFRAID
TO EXPRESS HER EMOTIONS.

I'M CRAZY ABOUT MY MOM
BECAUSE SHE CAN DO A
HUNDRED THINGS AT ONCE.

I'M CRAZY ABOUT MY MOM
BECAUSE SHE LETS US
HELP HER IN THE GARDEN.

I'M CRAZY ABOUT MY MOM
BECAUSE SHE STILL KNOWS HOW
TO BOOGIE TO THAT OLD MUSIC
SHE LIKES TO LISTEN TO.

I'M CRAZY ABOUT MY MOM
BECAUSE SHE MAKES ME FEEL
A WHOLE LOT BETTER
EVEN WHEN I'M SICK.

Oooops.

I'M CRAZY ABOUT MY MOM
BECAUSE SHE STAYS SO COOL
EVEN WHEN I GOOF UP A LITTLE.

I'M CRAZY ABOUT MY MOM
BECAUSE SHE KNOWS HOW
TO BRIGHTEN UP A RAINY DAY.

Yes, I'll read you another story tomorrow night.

I'M CRAZY ABOUT MY MOM
BECAUSE SHE IS THE WORLD'S
VERY BEST TUCKER-INNER.

I'M CRAZY ABOUT MY MOM
EVEN THOUGH SHE SOMETIMES
HAS TO GET TOUGH WITH US.

And you just wait until your dad gets home and hears what you've done.

I'M CRAZY ABOUT MY MOM
BECAUSE SHE ALWAYS, ALWAYS
BELIEVES IN ME.

I'M CRAZY ABOUT MY MOM
BECAUSE SHE SMELLS WONDERFUL.

I'M CRAZY ABOUT MY MOM
BECAUSE SHE KNOWS THAT EVEN
MOMS NEED HELP SOMETIMES.

I'M CRAZY ABOUT MY MOM
BECAUSE SHE'S CRAZY ABOUT ME!

I'M CRAZY ABOUT MY MOM
BECAUSE SHE IS MINE!

EVERY TIME I THINK
OF YOU, I GIVE
THANKS TO MY GOD.
I ALWAYS PRAY FOR
YOU, AND I MAKE
MY REQUESTS WITH
A HEART FULL
OF JOY. ~ St. Paul

PHILIPPIANS 1:3-4 NLT